Colorful CREATIONS

You Can Make and Share

by Mari Bolte

illustrated by Paula Franco

D1265386

CAPSTONE YOUNG READERS
a capstone imprint

Table of Contents

Pack your bags for fun with the Sleepover Girls! Every Friday, Maren, Ashley, Delaney, and Willow get together for crafts, fashion, cooking, and, of course, girl talk! Read the books, get to know the girls, and dive in to this book of cool projects that are Sleepover Girl staples!

Build a travel journal to record your favorite vacation, or make a gift box for your BFFs. Pocket magnets and itty bitty frames will make your Luke Lewis shrine (aka your "Luke-r") all yours. Express yourself with monograms and cheer on your home team with a homemade banner. Grab some glue, phone some friends, and start scrapbooking with your very own Sleepover Girls.

MEET THE SLEEPOVER GIRLS!

Willow Marie Keys

Patient and kind, Willow is a wonderful confidante and friend. (Just ask her twin, Winston!) She is also a budding artist with creativity for miles. Willow's Bohemian style suits her flower child within.

Maren Melissa Taylor

Maren is what you'd call "personality-plus"— sassy, bursting with energy, and always ready with a sharp one-liner. You'll often catch Maren wearing a hoodie over a sports tee and jeans. An only child, Maren has adopted her friends as sisters.

Ashley Francesca Maggio

Ashley is the baby of a lively Italian family. This fashionista-turned-blogger is on top of every style trend via her blog, Magstar. Vivacious and mischievous, Ashley is rarely sighted without her beloved "purse puppy," Coco.

Delaney Ann Brand

Delaney's smart, motivated, and always on the go! You'll usually spot low-maintenance Delaney in a ponytail and jeans (and don't forget her special charm bracelet, with charms to symbolize her Sleepover Girl buddies.)

Scrapbooked Scrapbook

Scrapbooks hold pages full of memories. But the outside should reflect who you are just as much as the inside. A few simple accessories will turn a boring scrapbook into one that's 100 percent you.

WHAT YOU'LL NEED

12-inch (30.5 centimeter) square scrapbook

two 15-inch (38 cm) pieces heavy-duty fabric

fabric glue

scissors or craft knife

butter knife or dowel

embellishments, such as stickers, charms, and ribbon

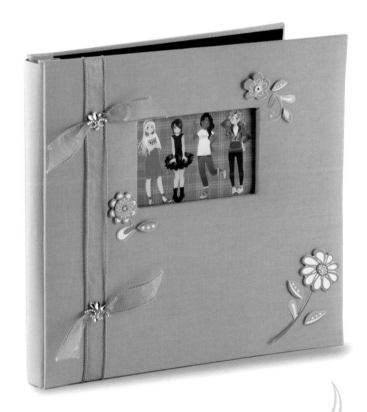

1 Open the scrapbook and locate the screws under the binding. Unscrew, and set the pages, spine, and screws aside.

2 Lay the fabric print side down on your workspace. Lay the front cover on the fabric.

3 Fold and glue the edges of the fabric over the back of the cover. Let dry completely.

4 Repeat Steps 2–3 for the back cover.

5 Use glue to cover the scrapbook's spine with fabric.

6 Use scissors or a craft knife to cut a rectangle shape inside the front cover's picture window. Leave about 1 inch (2.5 cm) of extra fabric all the way around.

7 Cut a small slit in each corner of the rectangular square. Use a small amount of glue on the underside of the fabric.

8 Use a butter knife or dowel to tuck the glued fabric around the edges of the picture window. Slide the knife into the photo pocket to prevent the pocket from being glued shut. Let dry completely.

9 Use glue to decorate the cover with embellishments. Reassemble scrapbook when ready to use.

Bedazzled Box

Willow has a serious crafter's kit. From decoupage glue to scrapbooking scissors, she's always ready to DIY it. Bling out your box of tricks so it's ready for your next colorful creation.

WHAT YOU'LL NEED

decorative paper, such as wrapping paper or scrapbook paper

cardboard box with lid

scissors

sponge brush

decoupage glue

1. Tear or cut used wrapping paper into small pieces. Place the cardboard box and lid on newspaper.

2. Dip a sponge brush in decoupage glue. Apply a thin layer of glue to the back of one wrapping paper piece.

3. Lay the piece flat on the box. Smooth out any wrinkles with your fingers.

4. Cover the piece of wrapping paper and surrounding area with another thin layer of decoupage glue.

5. Repeat steps 2-4 until the box and lid are covered with wrapping paper. Let dry for five minutes.

6. Apply a thin layer of decoupage glue over the entire box and lid. Let dry completely before placing the lid on the box.

Organizer Board

Maren loves decorating her "Luke-r"—er, locker—with a memory board full of Sleepover Girl treasures. Hang photos, postcards, and any other bits and pieces you want to remember.

WHAT YOU'LL NEED

12- by 17-inch (30.5- by 43-cm) piece of fabric

10- by 15-inch (25.4- by 38-cm) piece of thick cardboard

glue gun and hot glue

scissors

½-inch (1.3 cm) wide, 6 feet (1.8 meter) long piece of ribbon

thumbtacks

1 Lay the fabric pattern-side-down on your work surface. Lay the cardboard over the fabric and wrap it tightly around the back. Hot glue the fabric edges to the backside of the cardboard.

2 Cut ribbon into four 9-inch (23-cm) strips and two 18-inch (46-cm) strips. Arrange strips in a crisscross pattern on the front of the bulletin board.

3 Use thumbtacks to hold the ribbons in place where they cross.

4 Turn the board over. Pull the end of one ribbon tight to the back of the board and hot glue in place. Repeat with both ends of all ribbons.

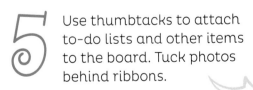

5 Use thumbtacks to attach to-do lists and other items to the board. Tuck photos behind ribbons.

Petite Portraits

Want to get your locker featured on Ashley's blog, Magstar? Get one accessory closer to her "Lockers You Wish You Had" entry with these itty bitty photo frames.

WHAT YOU'LL NEED

bottle caps

magazines

pen

scissors

cardstock or other heavy paper

clear glue

clear tape

super glue

toothpick

thin, self-adhesive magnets

1 Place a bottle cap on a small picture in a magazine. Trace around the cap with a pen, and cut out the picture.

2 Trace the bottle cap onto a piece of cardstock, and cut out the circle. Spread a small drop of glue on one side of the circle. Press the picture to the cardstock circle and let dry.

3 Cover the front of the picture with clear tape, making sure not to leave any gaps. The tape will keep the glue in Step 5 from soaking the paper. Trim off extra tape.

4 Carefully apply small drops of super glue to the raised circle inside the bottle cap. Be careful not to touch the glue with your fingers. Press the picture into the cap. Allow the super glue to dry.

5 Put a small amount of clear glue on the picture. Tilt the bottle cap around to spread the glue over the whole picture. If air bubbles form, use a toothpick to move the glue around. Let dry completely.

6 Peel off the adhesive liner from the back of a thin magnet. Press the magnet to the back of the bottle cap frame.

TIP:
You can also use photos of your friends or pets for this project. Use a computer to resize your images so they're small enough to fit inside the bottle caps. Then print the photos on photo paper.

Cute Coasters

Whether they're for decorations, gifts, or furniture protection, coasters are fun and easy! Leave your stamp on these cute coasters.

WHAT YOU'LL NEED

pencil

scissors

scrapbooking paper

ceramic tile

foam brush

decoupage glue

spray acrylic sealer

craft glue

small felt pads

1 Trace and cut out a piece of scrapbooking paper the same size as the tile.

2 Paint the tile with an even layer of decoupage glue.

3 Carefully press the paper onto the tile. Be sure to press out any bubbles. Let dry for 20 minutes.

4 Brush a thin layer of decoupage glue over the tiles. Let dry 15 minutes.

5 Repeat Step 4 two to three more times, waiting 15 minutes between each coat. After the final coat, let dry completely, at least overnight.

6 In a well-ventilated area, spray coaster with acrylic sealer. Let dry completely.

7 Glue felt pads to the bottom of the coaster. Let dry completely before using.

Travel Journal

Your mom may not be a travel mag editor like Maren's, but that doesn't mean you shouldn't remember your top vacays. Organize your memories in a totally tote-able travel journal.

WHAT YOU'LL NEED

scissors

postcards

cardstock

scrapbooking paper

photographs

cardboard

hole punch

decoupage glue and paintbrush

glue

binder rings

ribbon

1 Trim postcards, cardstock, and scrapbooking paper to match the size of your photos.

2 Trim cardboard to make a front and back cover. Punch holes in the front and back covers ½ inch (1.3 cm) from the top edge and 1 inch (2.5 cm) from the left edge.

3 Trim photos into small pieces. Brush front and back cover with decoupage glue. Arrange photos to create a mini gallery. Once photos are arranged to your liking, brush with at least three coats of decoupage glue. Let each coat dry for 15 minutes before applying the next.

4 Glue pages together so there's something on both the front and back. For example, glue the back of a photo to the back of a postcard, so the pictures on both face out. Or glue a piece of cardstock to the back of the postcard. Let glue dry completely before continuing.

5 Punch two holes in each page in the same locations as the front and back covers, using the front cover as a guide.

continued

6 Thread binder rings through the holes in the front cover. Add pages, then the back cover. Close the binder rings.

WHAT ELSE TO ADD?

There are dozens of ways to make this travel journal exclusively yours. Here are just a few ideas.

- Use the cardstock pages to record vacation memories. Write down your favorite song at the time, or what you ate each day. Use a pen with archival ink for durability.

- Glue in ticket stubs, fortunes from fortune cookies, maps, business cards, or stamps.

- Use watercolor or other art paper for pages. Paint or sketch scenes from your trip.

- Punch holes in bottle caps or smashed pennies and tie them to the binder rings. Or hang keychains, charms, or buttons off the rings.

- Glue small pieces of cardstock near the edge of the pages to create scalloped edges, tabs, or bookmarks.

- Use collected items, such as sand, dried flowers, or sea shells for texture.

Yours Always, Luke Lewis

For those who live and breathe their favorite movie or pop star, send a piece of Hollywood through the mail. Love always, Luke Lewis!

WHAT YOU'LL NEED

thin cardboard

thin wool batting

paper glue

printed paper, lightweight card stock, or other colorful paper

fine tip marker

double-sided adhesive tape

5x7-inch (13x18-cm) folded white card

continued

1 Cut out one 3x4-inch (8x10-cm) heart from a piece of cardboard. Do the same on a piece of batting. Glue the cardboard and batting heart together.

2 Cut one 5-inch (13-cm) square from a piece of paper. Cut several 2- and 3-inch (5- and 8-cm) squares from different papers. Glue the small squares onto the larger square in a random pattern. overlap and angle the small squares as desired. The small squares can go over the edges of the larger one. Top with a pic of your favorite celebrity, if desired.

3 Use a marker to draw faux stitches around the edges of all the pieces.

4 Turn your paper piece upside down. Center the cardboard heart on top of the paper, batting side down. Lightly trace around the heart shape on the paper.

5 Cut the heart shape from the paper, leaving ½ inch (1.3 cm) extra around the entire shape. Then cut slits around the edges of the paper heart, ending each slit at the guide line. Lay the paper heart on your workspace, patterned side down.

6 Apply tape around the edges of the cardboard heart. Lay this heart, tape side up, on the paper heart. Roll the paper slits over the edges of the cardboard to stick to the tape.

CREATE THE CARD

1 Cut long strips from different paper prints in varying widths. Position the strips on the front of the folded card, overlapping the edges slightly.

2 Glue the strips in place. When they're dry, trim edges to match with the edges of the card.

3 Use a marker to draw faux stitches around the edges of the strips.

4 Glue the heart to the front of the card.

Monogrammed Gift Bag

The Sleepover Girls know that Willow makes and gives the best gifts! They still talk about the monogrammed gift bag she made for Maren's half birthday. Make gift giving even more fun by making bags for all your friends.

WHAT YOU'LL NEED

plain gift bag

spray adhesive

paper doily

paintbrush

acrylic paint

unpainted wooden letter

stamp carving block

pencil

craft knife

1 Lay the gift bag flat on top of newspaper, and decide where you want the monogram to be.

2 Spray the rough side of the doily with adhesive. Press onto the part of the bag you want monogrammed. Paint around the inside edge of the doily. Do not paint outside the edges.

3 While paint is still wet, carefully remove the doily. Let paint dry completely.

4 Place the wooden letter on top of the stamp block. Make sure the letter is facing backwards so it stamps facing the correct way. Trace around the letter.

5 Use the craft knife to cut out the letter. If you're uncomfortable using the craft knife, ask an adult for help.

6 Dab a small amount of paint onto newspaper or another work surface. Use a foam brush to lightly dab some paint onto the stamp.

7 Center the stamp in the center of the doily print. Press down evenly, and then lift straight up. Let paint dry completely.

Go Tigers!

There's nothing Ashley loves more than cheering on her team, the Valley View Tigers (and especially her crush, Grant!) Get caught up in the game with this homemade home team banner.

WHAT YOU'LL NEED

pencil

scissors

cardstock

chalk

yellow felt, stiffened sheets

red felt, sticky-backed stiffened sheets

craft knife

letter stencils

gold sticky-back foam

ribbon

1 Draw and cut out a triangle shape from the cardstock.

2 Draw and cut out a slightly smaller triangle shape from the cardstock.

3 Use chalk to trace the larger template onto the yellow felt. Cut out eight triangles. Set aside.

4 Trace the smaller template onto the red felt. Cut out eight triangles. Set aside.

5 Trace and cut out letter stencils onto the back side of the foam. Trace the letters backward so they face the right direction when flipped over.

6 Remove the protective back from the foam letters. Stick a letter onto a red triangle. Repeat for the rest of the letters.

* 7 Remove the protective back from the red triangles. Stick a red triangle onto a yellow triangle.

8 Use the scissors to cut small slits at the top corners of each yellow triangle. Thread the ribbon through the slits to hang your banner.

Quilled *Letter*

Personalize your room with a monogram! Use paper quilling to give this classic letter a modern update.

WHAT YOU'LL NEED

acrylic paint

foam paintbrush

papier mache letter

quick-drying paper glue with fine-tip applicator

¼-inch (0.6-cm) wide quilling paper strips

slotted quilling tool

quilling needle

tweezers

1 Paint letter with acrylic paint. Let dry completely. Add a second coat of paint, if desired.

2 Fold one quilling strip in half width wise. Then tear it into two strips. Insert both strips into the slotted quilling tool.

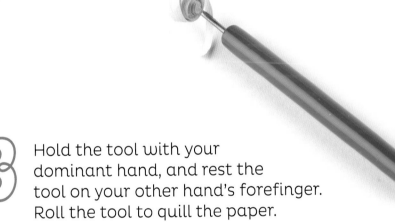

3 Hold the tool with your dominant hand, and rest the tool on your other hand's forefinger. Roll the tool to quill the paper.

4 When you get to the end, hold the rolled strips securely using your thumb and middle finger. Push the paper roll off the tool.

5 Using the quilling needle, apply glue to the rolled paper end. Press and hold until secure.

6 Repeat steps 2-5 to create several rolled strips. Be creative with the shapes. Some can be rolled completely. Roll just part of some strips, leaving a tail. Squeeze a rolled circle to create a teardrop. Keep some rolls tight, and let others get loose before gluing. Have fun!

LOTS OF CHOICE!

Quilling paper can be rolled into many different shapes. The color combinations and possible patterns are endless with even a few different quilling shapes.

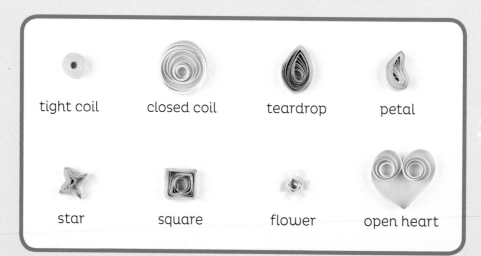

tight coil   closed coil   teardrop   petal

star   square   flower   open heart

7 Squeeze a small puddle of glue onto scrap paper. Carefully grab a quilled shape with tweezers and dip the bottom edges in glue.

8 Place the shape onto the letter. Gently press down on the shape with your fingers to secure. Repeat until the letter is as full as you want.

DIY Decals

Animal shelter pets, like Delaney's dog Frisco, need help finding their forever homes. These DIY wall decals will help your local shelter display pics of their adoptable animals. The best part? The shelter can change the photos as pets come and go.

WHAT YOU'LL NEED

photo

permanent markers

scissors

clear repositional vinyl contact paper

credit card or ruler

double-sided tape

1 Using the photo as a template, draw frames onto the front side of the contact paper. Draw a variety of frames, from fancy to simple.

2 Use scissors to cut out the frames.

3 Decide where to hang your frames. Peel away the edge of a frame's backing and position the frame in the desired location.

4 Slowly peel away the rest of the backing. Use the credit card or ruler to press down the frame and squeeze out any air bubbles.

5 Use double-sided tape to place a photo in the center of each frame.

Paper punch-outs bring
the Sleepover Girls to
life! From photo frames
and door hangers to
bookmarks and sticker
pages, you can bring
Maren, Delaney, Ashley,
and Willow wherever
you go.

USE PUNCH OUT FACES TO
ATTACH TO PARTY FAVORS ...

DECORATIONS, OR YOUR
OWN SLEEPOVER
INVITATIONS!

WOULD YOU RATHER

Qs about U

WOULD YOU RATHER

Qs about U 2

WOULD YOU RATHER

give it up

WOULD YOU RATHER

reality star

WOULD YOU RATHER

cash it in

WOULD YOU RATHER

social

Card 1

1. Would you rather start with appetizers or dessert?

2. Would you rather live in New York or San Francisco?

3. Would you rather go on a big adventure or stay curled up with a good book?

4. Would you rather always wear heavy boots and socks or go barefoot?

Card 2

1. Would you rather talk very slow or very fast?

2. Would you rather always oversleep or always be tired?

3. Would you rather have an extra finger or have only four?

4. Would you rather talk to someone on the phone or send them a text?

5. Would you rather always be alone or never be alone?

Card 3

1. Would you rather be a skillful dancer or a talented singer?

2. Would you rather be a reality or Internet sensation?

3. Would you rather have your life as a sitcom or a reality show?

4. Would you rather date a celebrity with a quiet life or a celebrity with his/her own reality show?

Card 4

1. Would you rather walk everywhere and be on time or run everywhere and always be late?

2. Would you rather give up salty or sweet foods?

3. Would you rather go without the Internet for a year or go without music for a month?

4. Would you rather listen to only male or only female musicians?

Card 5

1. Would you rather win tickets to Fashion Week or to the Super Bowl?

2. Would you rather date someone boring but super attractive or someone interesting and plain looking?

3. Would you rather improve your attractiveness or your intelligence?

4. Would you rather carry an ugly bag or wear ugly shoes?

Card 6

1. Would you rather have a boring job that paid well, or an interesting job with a small paycheck?

2. Would you rather have a super-fancy, expensive cell phone, or a super-fancy, expensive car?

3. Would you rather go on an exotic vacation with no spending money or a simple vacation with lots of cash to spare?

Favor BOX

You're Invited

TO A SLEEPOVER!

With: _____

Where: _____

When: _____

RSVP: _____

With: _____

Where: _____

When: _____

RSVP: _____

Thank You!

USE THESE STICKERS TO CUSTOMIZE
FAVORS, DECORATIONS OR YOUR
SLEEPOVER INVITATIONS!

sleepover Girls

Best Friends

You're Invited

Thank You!

Sticker FUN!

What's Your Memory Mojo?

Maren loves Luke Lewis—and she let the world know it with her super-creative scrapbook! What's your ideal way to display the things that matter to you? Find out your memory mojo with this handy-dandy quiz.

When you and your friends get together, you capture the important moments with:

a) a smartphone camera
b) a digital point-and-shoot camera
c) a video camera
d) a fancy SLR camera

Your favorite thing to do on a Friday night is:

a) go to a party
b) have a sleepover with friends
c) go to the movies
d) curl up with a good book

When you get an awesome set of photos, your first thought is:

a) "I can't wait to share these on Instagram!"
b) "Time to make a new Facebook album."
c) "How cool! Wonder if I could turn these into a slide show?"
d) "These will go perfectly with that beachy scrapbook layout I made."

If you ever became famous, your favorite part of being a star would be:

a) having millions of followers
b) having paparazzi document your every move
c) being in movies and TV shows
d) doing magazine interviews

How private are you about your social life?

a) My life is an open book!
b) I like sharing news and photos with a select group of peeps.
c) I pick and choose what I share with people.
d) I like to keep things somewhat private.

If I could learn anything tech-y in school, it would be:

a) coding
b) photography
c) video editing
d) graphic design

What's your fave way to display your photos?

a) using an app to create a collage
b) Fun with Flickr!
c) making a YouTube slide show
d) a good old-fashioned picture frame

What's your book style?

a) I go on Goodreads to see what everyone else is reading and pick my books that way.
b) I'm all about my e-reader.
c) I usually see the movie first and then read the book.
d) There's nothing better than a big stack of books!

The Sleepover Girl I relate to most is:

a) Ashley
b) Delaney
c) Maren
d) Willow

If you chose mostly "A" answers, your source of memory mojo is Social Media. Well, hello, Ms. Social Media Savvy! You're constantly sharing your pics with the world—and your followers "like" every minute of it. Your celeb twinsie: Kendall Jenner, whose life is an open book on social media for her gazillions of fans.

If you chose mostly "B" answers, your source of memory mojo is Digital Photos. Who needs an old-fashioned photo album when you can keep all your memories online? The digital domain is the way to go for you. Your celeb twinsie: Dianna Agron, who has said she buys a new camera every year and loves to digitally document her adventures on the set of *Glee*.

If you chose mostly "C" answers, your source of memory mojo is Filmmaking. All the world's a stage—and you love to document it. Making videos is the perfect way to do just that! Your celeb twinsie: Katy Perry, who put up $2 million of her own money to share her tour journey in the documentary flick *Part of Me*.

If you chose mostly "D" answers, your source of memory mojo is Scrapbooking. Pictures are forever, and you intend to keep them that way by preserving them in print. Your celeb twinsie: Taylor Swift, who's super-crafty and probably has a scrapbook (or 100!) on the shelf.

MAD LIB

Making a scrapbook
can be a hilarious trip down memory
lane. Just ask Maren! She got inspired one day
after making her Luke Lewis scrapbook and decided
to go through old photos. The first one she found made her
snort with laughter—it was a pic of her and Willow on the
_____ dressed as a _____ and _____.
[type of furniture]   [Halloween costume]   [Halloween costume]
Too cute! Next, she came across a picture of Ashley rocking out at their
school's karaoke fund-raiser, posing like_____ .
                                             [name of famous pop star]
(Maren could still hear her belting out "_____" in her head.)
                                            [name of song]
Then Maren unearthed a super-embarrassing one of her and Delaney at a
_____-eating contest with their faces smushed into
[type of food]
the_____ . Her stomach felt full just looking at it! Flipping through
   [food]
all the old pics, Maren had to smile—she and the Sleepover Girls
certainly had no shortage of memories. And now it was time to
preserve all of them in a scrapbook! Now for the big decision:
should she use a _____layout or a
                   [type of decoration]
_____ layout? A scrapbooker's
[type of decoration]
work is never done!

sleepover Girls

Join the fun by following Delaney, Maren, Ashley, and Willow's adventures in the Sleepover Girls series!

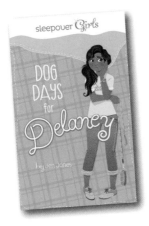

Then start the party with Sleepover Girls Crafts. Each book will show you how to replicate the fashions, crafts, and recipes created by the Sleepover Girls.

CRAFT IT ciy YOURSELF™

FUN & FABULOUS CRAFT AND ACTIVITY TITLES

for teens and tweens

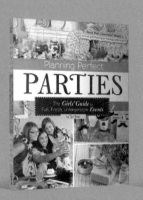

Planning Perfect **PARTIES**
The *Girls'* Guide to Fun, Fresh, Unforgettable *Events*

DESSERT DESIGNER
CREATIONS YOU CAN MAKE *and Eat!*
51 FUN CREATIONS Fun Enough For *Kids*

CUSTOM CONFECTIONS
DELICIOUS DESSERTS YOU CAN CREATE *and Style!*
40 FUN CREATIONS Easy Enough For *KIDS!*

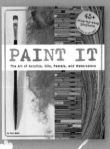

PAINT IT
The Art of Acrylics, Oils, Pastels, and Watercolors
45+ step-by-step projects

Paper Artist
Creations You Can Fold, Tear, Wear, or Share

Fashion FORWARD
Creating Your Look With the Best of Vintage Style

Fashion DRAWING STUDIO
A Guide to Sketching Stylish Fashions

Re-Craft
Unique Projects that Look Great (AND SAVE THE PLANET)

Capstone Young Readers are published by
Capstone, 1710 Roe Crest Drive, North Mankato,
Minnesota 56003.

www.capstoneyoungreaders.com

For information regarding permission, write to
Capstone, 1710 Roe Crest Drive, North Mankato,
Minnesota 56003.

Library of Congress Cataloging-in-Publication Data
Cataloging-in-publication information is on file with
the Library of Congress.
ISBN 978-1-62370-198-7 (paperback)

Designer: Tracy Davies McCabe
Craft Project Creators:
Kim Braun & Marcy Morin
Photo Stylist: Sarah Schuette
Art Director: Nathan Gassman
Production Specialist: Laura
Manthe

Photo Credits:
All Photos By Capstone Press:
Karon Dubke

Artistic Effects:
shutterstock

Printed in China.
032014   008081RRDF14